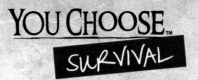

YOU CHOOSE™

SURVIVAL

P9-CRZ-374

Can You Survive

THE

JUNGLE?

An Interactive Survival Adventure

by Matt Doeden

Consultant:
Jim Penn
Associate Professor
Department of Geography and Planning
Grand Valley State University

CAPSTONE PRESS
a capstone imprint

You Choose Books are published by Capstone Press,
1710 Roe Crest Drive, North Mankato, Minnesota 56003.
www.capstonepub.com

Library of Congress Cataloging-in-Publication Data
Doeden, Matt.
  Can you survive the jungle? : an interactive survival adventure / by Matt Doeden;
Consultant, Jim Penn.
      p. cm.—(You choose: survival)
  Includes bibliographical references and index.
  ISBN 978-1-4296-6588-9 (library binding)
  ISBN 978-1-4296-7349-5 (paperback)
  1. Jungle survival—Juvenile literature. 2. Jungles—Juvenile literature.
I. Penn, Jim. II. Title.
  GV200.5.D64 2012
  613.6'909152—dc22   2011005320

Summary: Describes the fight for survival in the jungle.

Editorial Credits
Brenda Haugen, editor; Veronica Correia and Bobbie Nuytten, designers; Wanda
Winch, media researcher; Eric Manske, production specialist

Photo Credits
ageFOTOSTOCK: Reinhard H, 73; Alamy: BrazilPhotos.com/Ricardo Funari, 44,
Picture Contact BV, 6; Capstone Press: Gary Sundermeyer, 77 (all); Dreamstime:
clearviewstock, 56; iStockphoto: Ammit, 100, aricvyhmeister, 93, Jim Johnsen,
51, migin, 12, 16, Warwick Lister-Kaye, 28; James P. Rowan: 21, 38, 49, 55, 70, 95;
REUTERS: Jamil Bittar, 62, 66, 98; Shutterstock: 1971yes, 10, Ammit, 86, amybbb,
104, Andrew Bassett, 103, Dmitrijs Mihejevs, 40, Gustavo Frazao, 97, mikeledray, 19,
pashabo, Design Element, worldswildlifewonders, Cover

Printed in Eau Claire, Wisconsin.
002303

TABLE OF CONTENTS

About Your
ADVENTURE

YOU are lost in a dangerous place—the Amazon jungle. Predators prowl through the thick vegetation. Deadly snakes and spiders creep in dark places. Huge black caimans and electric eels lurk below murky waters. How will you survive?

In this book you'll deal with extreme survival situations. You'll explore how the knowledge you have and the choices you make can mean the difference between life and death.

Chapter One sets the scene. Then you choose which path to read. Follow the directions at the bottom of each page. The choices you make will change your outcome. After you finish one path, go back and read the others for new experiences and more adventures.

YOU CHOOSE the path you take through your adventure.

Small planes are often the only way to access remote areas of the world.

CHAPTER 1

Lost in the Jungle

You throw your backpack over your shoulder and wave to your parents before stepping aboard the small airplane. It's the end of summer vacation—time to head back to civilization and school.

You've spent an exciting summer living in the basin of the Amazon River in South America—the largest rain forest in the world. Your parents are photographers working on a book about the Amazon's huge variety of life. You've spent all summer in the hot, sticky jungle helping them find interesting plants, animals, and insects. You've even taken some photos with your own camera.

Turn the page.

But now the camera is tucked away in your backpack, along with your journal. You also brought a change of clothes, your trusty pocketknife, a bag of trail mix, and a bottle of water. The excitement of trekking through the Amazon with your parents is over. You wish you could finish the job with them, but they won't let you miss school.

You take your seat behind Maria, the airplane's pilot. She will fly you to Brazil's capital city, Brasilia. There you'll board a jet headed for home. You talk as the plane takes off, telling Maria about your adventures. But soon you close your eyes and drift off to sleep.

Suddenly you're awakened from a dream. The airplane is shuddering. You sit forward, startled. The plane's engine is making a horrible coughing noise. You can feel the plane descending.

"Chute!" Maria shouts, pointing to the back. "Put on your parachute! We're going down!"

You quickly grab one of the parachutes and begin strapping it to your back. You've done this before but never for a real emergency. Your fingers tremble as you work the straps, but you manage to put it on. You grab the other parachute and hand it to Maria, but she waves it away.

"Go!" she shouts. "There's no time! I'll try to find an open spot to land!"

You grab your backpack and do as you're told. You pull the door open. With only a small hesitation, you jump. As soon as you're clear of the plane, you pull your parachute's cord. The chute pops open, slowing your fall with a jolt. You turn and watch as the plane goes down in the distance.

Turn the page.

A parachute can carry you for many miles.

Your landing is rough. You're scraped and bruised from falling through the canopy of trees. Still, you were lucky. You're on the ground and alive. You wonder what happened to Maria. The plane was headed south. You look in that direction. From the jungle floor, you can't see more than 20 feet ahead.

Slowly, the reality of your situation hits you.
You're alone and lost in the jungle. You're certain
there will be a rescue search. But the Amazon
is huge. You can't just sit around and hope to be
rescued. As you see it, you have three choices.

To take off in search of rescue, turn to page **13.**

To build a camp and try to signal rescuers,
turn to page **39.**

To look for the plane and Maria, turn to page **67.**

It's easy to lose your direction in the green tangle of the jungle.

CHAPTER 2

On the Move

You've had some training in jungle survival. The best chance of finding rescue is to head downhill. Most villages lie along waterways. Water flows downhill, so that's the direction you should go.

There's no time to waste. Every minute you spend in the jungle alone is a minute of danger. You choose a direction that seems to be downhill and start moving.

The jungle is thick. You find a stick to clear away plants and branches as you move. The air is hot, humid, and filled with mosquitoes and other biting insects. Before long your water is gone. The ground is wet and muddy in many places, but there is no clear water available. You keep the empty water bottle, hoping to fill it up later.

13

Turn the page.

After hours of walking, you come upon a stream. It's not much—just a few feet wide—but it's something to follow. The stream's water looks clean. Your throat is dry, and you know that your body desperately needs water.

You fill your empty water bottle but hesitate before taking a drink. The water could contain tiny organisms that will make you sick. If you drink the water now, you could keep moving until sunset. Otherwise, you'd have to build a fire, heat the water to kill any dangerous organisms, and camp here for the night.

To drink the water now and keep moving, go to page 15.

To build a fire, heat the water, and camp here, turn to page 18.

You're starting to feel dizzy. You need water right away. You remember a trick you saw on TV where someone used T-shirt material as a crude water filter. You wrap layers of your T-shirt around the mouth of the bottle and let the water pass through it. You don't know if it will make a difference, but it couldn't hurt.

You take a deep breath and drink. The water is warm but refreshing. You find yourself gulping it down. You empty the bottle and refill it. Now you're ready to keep going.

You follow the stream down, knowing that it will likely lead to a larger river. An hour or two later, that's exactly what you find. The stream empties into a river that's at least 50 feet wide. You're thrilled to have found a major waterway. By following this river, you're likely to find people.

Turn the page.

Even water that looks clean can contain dangerous organisms.

But the sun is starting to set. You'll have to camp for the night. You have little time to build a proper shelter. You gather some branches and drape leaves over the top. You build the shelter up and away from the river. A rainstorm could cause a flash flood, so you need to keep some distance from the water.

It's a rough night of sleep. You're uncomfortable. You constantly feel things crawling on you. Late in the night, you're gripped by terrible stomach cramps and diarrhea. It must have been the water.

By daybreak you feel awful. The idea of fighting through the jungle, the heat, and the humidity is almost too much. You're not sure you can move far without passing out. All you want to do is lie in the shade and wait for someone to find you.

To get up and continue searching for rescue, turn to page **21.**

To stay and hope someone finds you, turn to page **23.**

Drinking water straight out of a jungle stream could be a terrible mistake, no matter how thirsty you are. Instead you use the remaining hours of daylight to build a shelter and a fire. The shelter is just a simple lean-to built with sticks and branches and covered with leaves.

To build a fire, you gather small sticks and any other dry material you can find, including some pages from your journal. You remove the lens of your camera. The powerful lens focuses the sun's light to a small point. This creates intense heat, which lights the paper and starts the fire.

Carefully you build the small flame into a roaring blaze. Next you use one of your shoelaces to tie the water bottle to a stick propped above the fire. The bottle is high enough above the flame that the plastic won't melt but close enough to heat the water. You know that the water doesn't have to boil to be purified. It only needs to get hot enough to kill any bacteria or parasites living in it.

Encircling a fire with rocks helps keep it contained.

Soon you're gulping clean, safe water. You refill the bottle and repeat the process so you have more water for tomorrow.

After munching some trail mix, you lie down for the night. You don't sleep much, but aside from nagging insects, nothing disturbs your little shelter.

Turn the page.

At daybreak you take off again. You follow the stream downhill to where it joins a river. The river is fairly large, with what looks like a strong current. A raft might carry you downstream quickly. But you would risk running into a caiman, anaconda, or other water predator. You then see what appears to be a trail of smoke far off in the distance, upstream from the river. The smoke could be coming from a village, but it might be miles away.

To travel by foot upstream, turn to page 24.

To build a raft and try to float downriver, turn to page 26.

The last thing you want to do right now is to get up and start moving again. But you know that if you give up now, you're dead. Your stomach is full of harmful bacteria or parasites, and you don't have much time. You must use what little strength you have to search for rescue.

You move back toward the river. With luck, you'll find a village downstream.

Many villages are located along rivers and streams, where water is abundant.

Turn the page.

As you stumble weakly along the riverbank, you notice a large log near the water's edge. You might be able to roll it into the water and use it to ride the current. That would get you downstream a lot faster. But it's also a risk. You might not have the strength to hold onto the log, especially if the current is strong. Or you could become caiman bait.

To try using the log to float down the river, turn to page **29**.

To continue on foot, turn to page **31**.

You feel terrible. The water you drank must have been loaded with bacteria and parasites. They're churning in your stomach now, making you too sick to do much of anything.

You lie down in your makeshift shelter. Later in the morning, a rain shower passes through. You know you should try to collect some of the fresh rainwater, but you don't have the energy.

Over the rest of the day, you grow weaker. By nightfall you're drifting in and out of consciousness. All you can do is hope that rescuers can somehow find you here. But in your heart, you know that's not going to happen.

THE END

To follow another path, turn to page 11.
To read the conclusion, turn to page 101.

Smoke could mean people, so that's the direction you go. You sling your backpack over your shoulder and start walking. After an hour or so, you notice the riverbanks are steeper and rockier. You also begin to hear a faint rumbling.

Soon you realize why. You look up to see a waterfall straight ahead of you.

"Oh no," you mumble to yourself.

The river crashes down over a small wall of rock. This cliff extends to both sides of the river, forming a barrier. You're not willing to double back and find another way around. That would take far too long.

You notice a spot where the rock face is sloped more gently. It looks like you could try climbing it. But without a rope, any slip could mean disaster. If you want to continue upstream toward the smoke trail, though, it's your only choice.

Maybe going downstream was the better idea after all. You could build a raft to help make up some of the time you lost following the smoke on foot.

To build a raft and go downstream, turn to page 26.

To try to climb the rock wall, turn to page 33.

You set down your backpack and get to work. The jungle provides you with everything you need to build a raft. You snap off tree limbs and small tree trunks and line them up. Next you collect some of the vines that grow all over the Amazon's trees. You strip the vines of their leaves and soak them in river water. The wet vines make great rope.

You use the vines to tie together the wood that forms the base of your raft. The project takes most of the day. A late-morning rain shower cools you off and provides some fresh drinking water.

Soon your raft is finished. It's not strong enough to survive any rapids, so you'll need a way to steer to shore if you come upon some. You grab a long stick to push yourself downriver and to steer when needed.

Late in the afternoon, you launch the raft and climb aboard. It supports your weight. Water seeps up through the cracks, but the raft keeps your body out of the water and away from predators. You push yourself out to the middle of the river and let the current take you. Soon you're floating downriver at a good pace. You're tired, hungry, and thirsty, but you're moving.

Turn the page.

Not long after you've started, you spot something ahead. A large black caiman sits in the shallow water along one of the banks. He's watching you. Caimans are fast swimmers. You have no doubt he could easily catch you before you pass by. Your heart races as the reptile slowly begins moving in your direction.

Male black caimans can grow to more than 13 feet long.

To use your pole to head for land on the opposite river bank, turn to page **35**.

To continue downriver, turn to page **36**.

Getting into a river with nothing but a log is a terrible risk. But you're sick, and time is not on your side. If you're going to survive, you have to take big risks.

The log is heavy, but you manage to roll it into the river. The current is weaker at the river's edge, so you walk the log out to waist-deep water. You try to climb onto the log, but it won't support your weight. You'll just have to hold onto it. You don't like leaving your lower body dangling in unfamiliar waters, but you have little choice.

In the middle of the river, the current is stronger. You cling to the log and watch as the jungle goes by. Within just a few minutes, you're already far from your starting place. It would have taken you hours to travel the same distance by foot.

Turn the page.

By afternoon a blistering sun beats down on you. You're dizzy and having trouble concentrating. Your body is still fighting whatever bacteria or parasites you drank, but it's losing the fight. All you can think about is holding onto the log.

Your river soon joins with a larger river. And then you hear voices. You look up and can hardly believe your eyes—you see a boat! Weakly, you try to signal the people aboard, but they've already spotted you. A man throws a life preserver in your direction.

You let go of the log and grab the life preserver. You've made it! You're still very sick, but you know that with some medical help, you'll make a full recovery.

THE END

To follow another path, turn to page 11.
To read the conclusion, turn to page 101.

Travel by foot may be slow and tiring, but at least you won't be at the mercy of a wild river. You fight your way through the heavy vegetation on the riverbank. Rain begins to fall. You collect some rainwater as it drips down from the canopy of trees above. At least this water is pure. You drink a little but vomit it up just a few minutes later.

Your pace is slowing. Painful stomach cramps make you stop and double over several times. Fighting through the jungle is hard work, and you just don't have the strength to do it.

By the afternoon, the sun is beating down mercilessly on your skin. You keep moving, unwilling to give up. But your body is failing. The heat is too much. Darkness is creeping around the edges of your vision. Your head feels light. Too late, you realize that you're about to faint.

Turn the page.

Slowly the world comes back into focus. You realize you must have fainted and hit your head, which is slick with blood. You're not entirely sure where you are. Weakly, you call out to your parents. You can't understand why they don't answer.

Your head feels like it's spinning. You close your eyes. You tell yourself that it's just for a moment. But part of you understands that you won't be opening them again.

THE END

To follow another path, turn to page 11.
To read the conclusion, turn to page 101.

You start up the cliff, finding handholds and footholds in the sharp, jagged rock. The rocks are also wet and slippery, so you have to be careful with each move.

Slowly you work your way up the rock face. You're more than halfway there, and now you can use exposed tree roots as handholds. You grab onto a root and use it to pull yourself up. But as you lunge up with one foot, the root snaps off in your hand. Desperately, you grab for another handhold, but it's too late.

You hit the rock below with a sickening crunch. You black out momentarily from the pain. Sometime later you regain consciousness. You can't feel one arm and know it must be broken. You can see a jagged piece of bone jutting out of one leg. And the back of your head is matted with blood.

Turn the page.

Somehow you survived the fall. But with several broken bones and a head injury, you know that your survival will be short-lived. You took a risk, and you're going to pay the ultimate price. With your one working arm, you reach into your pack for your journal and pen and scrawl, "Good-bye."

THE END

To follow another path, turn to page 11.
To read the conclusion, turn to page 101.

Black caimans are lightning-quick in the water, so you think you have a better chance on land. Frantically you push yourself to the opposite shore. Your raft scrapes against the river bottom. You step off, pulling the raft behind you. You look over your shoulder. The huge reptile is still on the opposite shore. It's no longer watching you.

Relieved, you take a deep breath. That's when you notice a flash of motion out of the corner of your eye.

You didn't stop to think that where there's one black caiman, there might be more. In your panic you've steered almost right into the jaws of another caiman. The attack happens so quickly that you barely have time to regret your decision.

THE END

To follow another path, turn to page 11.
To read the conclusion, turn to page 101.

For all you know, there could be another caiman on the opposite shore. All you can do is continue. You hold your breath as the huge reptile slips below the water's surface. Your heart races. Your hands are shaking. Where is it? It could be right below your raft.

A minute passes. Then another. Your heartbeat slows. The caiman isn't coming after you. Perhaps it wasn't hungry. Or maybe the raft didn't look like food from below. Either way, you're alive and you're safe—for now.

The river soon flows into a still larger river. The sun is getting low in the sky, but you want to go just a bit farther before pulling to shore.

You're rewarded for your determination. In the distance, you see faint lights. The current carries you toward a small village. Several men are fishing on the riverbank.

"Help!" you shout to them. Two of the men jump into their boat and row to you. They pull you to safety. The villagers have a small two-way radio that you use to contact the police. You tell them to send rescuers immediately to search for Maria and the crashed airplane.

You've made it. You've survived the Amazon and all of its dangers. And what a story you'll have to tell your friends at home!

THE END

To follow another path, turn to page 11.
To read the conclusion, turn to page 101.

Caves and crevices can offer some protection from the weather.

CHAPTER 3

Making Camp

It won't be long before someone realizes your plane is missing. Maria filed a flight plan with the national aviation authority. That means rescuers will have an idea of where to look for you. The best thing you can do is to find a place to build a shelter. When rescuers come, you'll be ready.

To the west, the ground slopes upward. You want to camp on high ground. Heavy rains are frequent in the Amazon, and you never know where a flash flood might occur. High ground will be at much lower risk. Signaling rescuers will be easier from there too.

Turn the page.

You fold your parachute and sling it over your right shoulder. Its weight will slow you down, but it might be useful in building a shelter.

Mosquitoes and other insects swarm around you as you move through the jungle. You step carefully. A venomous snake could be waiting under any fallen log. The sounds of the jungle surround you— buzzing insects, jumping fish, and rustling leaves.

Piranhas are a danger in Amazon waters. These fish have razor-sharp teeth.

After about an hour, you come upon several large boulders. They form a small clearing in the jungle. This might be as good a spot for a camp as you'll find.

It's now late afternoon. There's much to do before sunset. You'll need a sturdy shelter to protect you from the weather. But you'll also need food and water. You've already gone through most of your water. You'll need to find another water source quickly.

To build a shelter, turn to page 42.

To search for food and water, turn to page 44.

Shelter is your top priority. You've still got your bag of trail mix. That can be your meal for the night.

This is where dragging your parachute through the jungle will pay off. You find two small trees about 10 feet apart. With your knife, you cut several of the cords on the parachute. After tying them together, you tie each end to one of the trees. Next you cut away a section of the parachute fabric. You drape this over the cords and then secure the ends to the ground. This forms a crude A-shaped tent. It isn't much to look at, but it will keep you dry at night.

Then you gather several medium-sized, straight branches. You lay them down in your shelter for a makeshift bed. The branches won't get you far off the ground, but they might keep away some of the insects crawling along the jungle floor.

You're exhausted by the time the shelter is finished. The sun is quickly setting. You try to start a fire by rubbing sticks together, but you get nowhere. So you go to bed without a fire and put up with the merciless mosquito attack. It's a long and miserable night, but it could be much worse.

The next morning you grab your pocketknife and head out into the jungle. You find an inga tree with some nearly ripe fruit. You gulp the delicious fruit hungrily.

Turn to page 56.

All that walking has made you hungry, and you want to keep up your strength. You set down your backpack and head back into the jungle. You know that buriti palm fruits, sweet inga fruits, and other fruits grow naturally in the Amazon.

Buriti palms produce small fruit with scaled skins.

As you move through the jungle, you carefully watch all around you. You come across a trampled area that looks like some sort of animal trail. There are tracks in the mud alongside the trail. You're not sure, but they look like peccary tracks. If you could kill a peccary, you'd have food to last you many days. But hunting is a risky choice. Peccaries can easily injure or kill a person.

To continue to forage for fruit, turn to page **46.**

To hunt for a peccary, turn to page **48.**

Your mouth waters at the thought of freshly roasted meat, but you decide against hunting. You'd have to use a lot of energy with no guarantee of getting your prey. Even if you did kill an animal, cooking it over an open fire might attract jaguars.

The jungle offers plenty of food with less risk. If you can't find fruit, you can always turn to beetle grubs. You've seen survival experts eat them on TV. They look disgusting, but you're willing to do whatever it takes to survive.

Luckily you don't have to resort to eating grubs. You find a stand of buriti palm trees. One palm has dropped fruit that's almost ripe. You collect several pieces of fruit. You use your knife to peel off the tough, scaly outer covering, so you can eat the yellow flesh. The half-ripe fruit tastes great.

The sun is nearing the horizon, so you head back to camp. There's no time to build a proper shelter or a fire. Instead you wrap yourself up in your parachute. It's a long, miserable night. With no fire or proper shelter, the mosquitoes are relentless. You sleep very little and wake up sore and tired.

You're not going to spend another night like that. It's time to build a shelter. You run some of the cord from your parachute between two trees. Then you drape your parachute cloth over it, forming a crude tent. Now you've got shelter and food. Things are looking up.

Turn to page 56.

You can't resist the idea of grilling meat over a campfire. You find a long branch and sharpen the end with your knife, making a crude spear. With the spear in hand, you quietly follow the tracks.

After several minutes you hear a rustling up ahead. Something large is moving in the dense vegetation. It might be the peccary. You move forward carefully.

Suddenly the rustling stops. Your prey has heard you. You charge forward. But whatever it is you're chasing darts away under the cover of the jungle.

To continue your chase, go to page **49**.

To give up and return to camp, turn to page **51**.

You follow, unwilling to give up. You dash through the jungle. Leaves, branches, and vines whack you in the face. Suddenly you find yourself sprawling forward. Your foot has caught on a root. You crash onto the ground, opening a wide gash in your head.

The jungle is full of many hazards, including exposed tree roots.

Turn the page.

You black out for a moment. When you regain consciousness, there's a sharp, throbbing pain in your right leg. You look down to see your ankle wrenched at an awful angle. You try to move it but almost black out again from the pain.

Your ankle is broken. You can't walk or even stand. You're lying alone in a thick jungle. You have no food, no water, no supplies, and no shelter. And worst of all, you have no hope.

You feel suddenly tired. You're losing lots of blood, and your body was already dehydrated. You know if you close your eyes, you may never open them again.

You fight to stay conscious. But you've lost too much blood. It's a fight you won't win.

THE END

To follow another path, turn to page 11.
To read the conclusion, turn to page 101.

You know better than to go running after unknown prey in the jungle. You tried to get meat, but you failed. It's time to head back and work on your shelter.

Peccaries are less than 3 feet long and can weigh more than 60 pounds.

Turn the page.

You start heading back the way you came, but after a few minutes, nothing looks familiar. The sun is quickly setting, so you know which direction is west. But your camp isn't where you thought it would be.

You double back again. With every turn you get more lost and confused. The sky is growing darker and darker. Soon you can barely see more than a few feet in front of you. You're desperate to find your camp. But in the dark, you might only get more confused. Maybe you should climb a tree and spend the night here, off the ground.

To climb a tree for the night, go to page 53.

To continue your search in the dark, turn to page 54.

There's nothing more you can do in the dark. It's time to get off the ground and out of reach of predators. You find a solid tree branch and pull yourself up. You don't dare fall asleep. But at least you're not on the damp ground, surrounded by snakes, spiders, and other creatures.

At sunrise, you lower yourself to the jungle floor. You think your camp is to the west, so you head in the direction opposite of the sun. Within 20 minutes, you reach your camp. You plop down on the ground and munch on some trail mix. Then you start work on a shelter. You're not spending another night without one.

Turn to page 56.

Your camp has to be around here somewhere. You just have to keep searching.

After about 20 minutes, the jungle is completely dark. You fumble along through the brush, feeling your way more than seeing. You stumble over a tree root, sprawling to the ground. You try crawling, but as you put your right hand forward, you feel a sharp, hot pain in your wrist.

You jerk your arm back. Something bit you, probably a snake. You stand, wiping the tears from your face. Your wrist feels strange. It pulses and starts to feel numb. Soon the feeling spreads farther up your arm.

The bite was venomous. Clutching your chest, you fall to your knees. You can't breathe. You gasp, but your lungs won't take any air. You black out and fall to the jungle floor. That's where you die, alone in the jungle.

The tree boa
can inflict a
painful bite.

THE END

To follow another path, turn to page 11.
To read the conclusion, turn to page 101.

Later in the morning, a rain shower passes through. You collect water as it drips down your parachute. You fill your bottle to the brim.

The Amazon averages more than 7 feet of rain each year.

You consider your priorities. You have food, shelter, and some water. Now you need to figure out a way to signal any rescuers. You expect airplanes and helicopters will be looking for you and Maria.

Your camp is in a natural clearing, so that will help. You just need a way to get the rescuers' attention. You could spell out the word "HELP" with wood and branches. But what are the odds that rescuers would see it?

The other option is to build a signal fire. You'd need a big blaze with lots of smoke. You're not sure you can build such a big fire by yourself.

To prepare a signal fire, turn to page 58.

To use wood to spell out a cry for help, turn to page 59.

You start by collecting the driest wood you can find. You arrange three large pieces in a pyramid. This will form the base of your fire. Underneath, you add smaller branches and pages from your journal as kindling.

The drier wood will burn hot, but it won't create a lot of smoke. You need green, wet wood and vegetation for that. You use your pocketknife to cut living branches off nearby trees. These branches are full of moisture. Finally you add a layer of green leaves and vegetation. They will burn slowly, but they'll release huge amounts of smoke.

Your fire is ready to light by late afternoon.

*To light the fire now, turn to page **61**.*

*To wait until you hear an aircraft, turn to page **64**.*

You imagine rescuers seeing a huge "HELP" from the air. There would be no mistaking that message because Brazilian pilots are trained to communicate in basic English. You collect long branches, carefully laying them out to form each letter. Soon you're dripping with sweat from dragging heavy wood around. But by the time you're done, you're pleased with your signal. Now you just need someone to see it.

Late that afternoon, you hear something from above. It's the sound of distant helicopter blades. It must be the search-and-rescue team!

You hurry to the clearing, shouting and waving your arms. But the hum of the helicopter soon fades away. It returns later, but it never comes close.

Several times during the next few days you hear the sound of an aircraft. It never comes close enough to spot your sign. Then the sounds stop. The search has probably ended. You realize that from the air your sign would hardly be noticeable in the dense jungle.

No one is going to find you here. You get ready to start walking. You're weak and tired. You're not sure you'll make it far. But it's the only chance you have. You won't stop fighting.

THE END

To follow another path, turn to page 11.
To read the conclusion, turn to page 101.

There's no telling when rescuers might come. You have got to send your signal now. You can always build another signal fire later if nobody spots this one.

You pull your camera from your backpack and carefully remove the lens. The lens is a powerful way to focus the sun's rays onto a single point. You focus the sunlight onto some tinder. In a few seconds, the tinder begins to smoke and catches fire. You carefully tend the flame, helping it to spread.

Within a few minutes, the fire's base is burning. It takes a lot longer before the wet vegetation starts to burn. But when it does, it releases big, billowing plumes of smoke. The smoke rises above the jungle canopy.

Turn the page.

You continue to feed the fire, adding both wood and green vegetation to keep the smoke coming. As you're trudging through the jungle looking for more wood, you hear something in the distance.

You rush to the clearing. The noise is getting louder. You let out a shout as you realize it's a helicopter. Your signal fire has worked!

It's difficult from the air to see a person in the jungle.

You're going to be rescued! You will have the helicopter pilot search for Maria too.

The jungle can be a scary, deadly place. But you stayed calm and remained focused on the goal of surviving. You proved that you have what it takes to stay alive.

THE END

To follow another path, turn to page 11.
To read the conclusion, turn to page 101.

You don't want to waste your signal fire if there's nobody around. You decide to wait until you hear something in the air before you light it.

While you wait, you head out into the jungle to find water. You come upon a small stream, where you fill your water bottle. You can take this water back to camp. There you'll heat it and make it safe to drink. As you head back to camp, you hear a distant buzzing. It's an aircraft! Rescuers are searching for you!

You rush back to where you've prepared your signal fire. Your hands are shaking as you pull the lens from your camera and use it to focus the sun's rays on your tinder. It takes a few moments, but the fire soon begins to burn. The dry wood burns first. But it doesn't release much smoke. You need the wet vegetation to burn.

It seems like you're waiting forever. Your heart is racing. Finally, the green wood starts to burn and smoke. But by the time it does, you don't hear the aircraft anymore.

You tend the fire for the rest of the afternoon, adding wood and vegetation. But you don't hear another plane. You'll try again tomorrow. But you're terrified that you may have missed your only chance. It's going to be a long, lonely night. You know you'll have to keep building fires every day until someone finds you.

THE END

To follow another path, turn to page 11.
To read the conclusion, turn to page 101.

A plane's wreckage may contain items that help in survival.

CHAPTER 4

In Search of Maria

You're alive and safe, but you don't know about Maria. If she's still alive, she's probably hurt and needs your help. Plus a crashed airplane may be easy for rescuers to spot. You might even be able to use its radio to call for help.

You don't know how far away the plane might be. Moving through the thick jungle will be dangerous and slow. But you've got to find Maria and then wait for rescue.

You have an idea of the direction to go, but you're not positive. Ahead of you stands a tall tree. It towers above the rest of the trees in the area. If you climb it, you might get a better idea of which direction to walk.

Turn the page.

But climbing a tree is a risk. Biting bala ants are often in trees, and you could slip and fall. A branch could break from your weight. Suffering any serious injury out here could be a death sentence.

Still the tree looks solid. And you'd hate to head off in the wrong direction.

*To take a risk and climb the tree, go to page **69**.*

*To rely on your sense of direction and stay on the ground, turn to page **72**.*

The jungle is a big place. If your sense of direction is even a little off, you might never find Maria and the plane. In this situation, you feel like you have to take some risks. You set your parachute at the bottom of the tree.

The lower half of the tree is quite solid, and you're a good climber. You don't see any biting ants. You're moving up without much trouble. But as you near the top, the branches are thinner. You slowly inch up the tree, carefully testing each branch to see if it will hold your weight. Snap! A branch breaks and tumbles to the jungle floor below. You catch yourself with your other hand, but the close call sends your heart racing.

Turn the page.

Soon you can climb no higher. You look out and can barely see over the jungle canopy. Far off in the distance, you see a trail of smoke. That has to be the plane! You note the position of the afternoon sun and climb back down. Now you know where to go. You can even see where the jungle thins a bit. You plan your route to avoid the heavy vegetation.

Bala ants will sting to protect their nests.

You start moving. It's hot and humid, and mosquitoes are constantly in your face, but you're making good progress. After a few hours, you reach one of the clearings you spotted from the tree. This looks like a good place to camp for the night. The sun will be setting soon.

To make camp, turn to page **77**.

To continue your search through the night, turn to page **81**.

It's far too early to be taking a risk such as climbing a tree. Besides, you have an idea of where to go. You head off through the thick vegetation, using a stick to hack at leaves as you move. The growth is so thick in spots that you have to turn around and find another way. At times it seems as if you're making no progress at all.

Soon you come upon a small river. It is shallow, but its water is dark and murky. You could follow it upstream, since it heads in the general direction you're going. But steep banks lie on either side of the river. You'd have to wade through the water to follow it.

You'd make much better progress, but the idea of walking through the murky water is scary. You don't know what's waiting beneath the surface. You imagine caimans with their powerful jaws or an electric eel that could shock you unconscious, causing you to drown.

Electric eels shock to kill prey, as well as in self-defense.

Your other choices aren't much better. You've been walking through the jungle for hours. You doubt you're much closer to the plane than when you started.

To continue by land, turn to page **74**.

To try traveling by river, turn to page **75**.

There's no way you're setting foot in that river. If there are predators around, it could be a death trap. You'll take your chances with the thick jungle.

You move alongside the river, pushing through the brush. After a few hours, you find that the going is easier. You come to a small clearing. The sun is getting low in the sky. Knowing that you have only an hour or two before sunset, you decide to make camp for the night.

Turn to page 77.

At the rate you're going, you'll never reach Maria. It's time to take a risk. Before getting into the water, you find a short, fat log that has fallen to the jungle floor. It will serve as a float in case you find deeper water ahead. You check your pack, take a sip from your water bottle, and head into the water.

The water is surprisingly warm. The current is weak, so moving upstream is fairly easy. As you hoped, you're finally covering some distance. It's not exactly in the direction you want to move, but it's close enough.

As you cling to your log, you start to get an uneasy feeling. The water here is deep. You can't even touch bottom. Suddenly, no more than 25 feet away, you notice a pair of eyes just above the water's surface watching you. It's a huge black caiman!

Turn the page.

To your horror, the eyes slip below the water's surface. A few seconds later, the huge caiman slams its powerful jaws down on your leg. Pain shoots through your entire body. The animal pulls you beneath the water's surface. In your panic, you gasp for air. But all you get is a lungful of murky river water. The caiman is going to win this battle.

THE END

To follow another path, turn to page 11.
To read the conclusion, turn to page 101.

The first thing you need is a fire. You gather dry wood, dead leaves, and pages from your journal, which you use as tinder. You cover the tinder with kindling made up of twigs and small branches. You add bigger sticks and small logs as fuel. Using your camera's lens, you focus the sun's rays on the tinder. Soon you have a roaring fire.

Tinder, kindling, and fuel

Turn the page.

But there's no time to build a shelter before the sun goes down. You sit up all night by your fire. You don't sleep, but at least you're safe.

The next morning you start out again. A morning rain shower allows you to collect water. You use leaves to funnel the water into your water bottle and your mouth. Then you continue along. You come upon a ridge, which gives you a good view of what's ahead. Then you see it. There's a black, smoking clearing in the jungle where the airplane went down. You can even see part of the plane. It's not far ahead.

Within a few hours, you reach the crash site. Pieces of the airplane are scattered about, but the cockpit is intact. With a deep breath, you force open the door and step inside.

"Help," whispers a hoarse voice. It's Maria! She's alive!

"I'm here, Maria!" you cry.

You find Maria still in the pilot's seat. She has a wide gash in her head. Her face is crusted with dried blood. One of her arms appears to be broken. Her skin is hot, red, and dry. You think she's dehydrated. She seems to be drifting in and out of consciousness.

"Here," you say. "Drink this."

You help her drink what water you have left, but it's barely a couple of swallows. She needs a lot more than that.

Turn the page.

The cockpit is like a sauna. The metal of the airplane traps the heat, and there's no breeze. You're afraid that Maria might not last much longer in here. But moving someone who has a broken bone or a spinal injury can cause even worse damage.

To move Maria outside to a shady spot, turn to page **83**.

To try to make her more comfortable without moving her, turn to page **87**.

You don't feel like you have the time to waste on making camp and sleeping. The clock is ticking, and you'll keep searching.

The jungle gets dark fast—even before the sun goes down entirely. Soon you can't see more than a few feet in front of you. You trudge through the thick brush. A branch smacks you hard in the face.

"Ouch!" you yelp, trying to hold back tears.

You stumble over roots and fallen logs. Before long you can't even tell which direction you're headed.

As you move slowly though the jungle, you hear flowing water. There must be a river ahead! You move in that direction, picking up your pace.

Turn the page.

You take a step, but there's no ground underneath. The false step sends you head over heels down a steep, rocky bank. It all happens so fast that you don't even have time to scream. Your neck breaks as you hit a shallow rock in the small river below. Your jungle adventure has a terrible ending.

THE END

To follow another path, turn to page 11.
To read the conclusion, turn to page 101.

You've spent enough time in the jungle to recognize heatstroke. Moving someone who is injured is a risk, but leaving Maria in the cockpit would be a death sentence.

Symptoms of Heatstroke

- Body temperature of 105 degrees Fahrenheit or higher

- Hot, red, dry skin

- Rapid pulse

- Rapid breathing

- Dizziness

Turn the page.

You run out of the cockpit and grab two long, straight tree branches and some vines. You lay the branches on your parachute and use the vines to tie the cloth to the branches, forming a crude stretcher. You then use more vines to tie Maria's body to the stretcher, so she won't fall as you move her. She groans as you move outside but doesn't say anything. You find a shaded spot and lay her down.

"I'll be back," you promise. "I need to find water for us."

You head back into the wreckage of the plane. Maria had a cooler with some snacks and beverages for the flight. As you search, you come across an emergency kit with some flares. You tuck them into your pocket. They might come in handy later.

The cooler is jammed under the pilot's seat. You grab it and rush outside. You take out a bottle of water and give Maria a few drops. She's still not fully conscious, so you are careful not to give her too much.

As evening approaches, Maria begins to come around. She's groggy but is able to talk.

"The airplane's radio is broken, but I might be able to fix it," she says. "I'll try in the morning."

"It's definitely worth a shot," you reply.

You build a fire for the evening, using one of the plane's emergency flares to start it. You find cans of beans in among the plane's supplies and cook them over the fire.

"I'm sure we'll be rescued soon," you tell Maria.

Just then you hear movement in the brush, followed by a loud growl. It's a jaguar!

You could rush into the airplane for protection, but Maria needs help. You're not sure if you'd make it. Maybe you could scare the big cat away instead.

Turn the page.

Jaguars are fast and can swim and climb trees.

To help Maria and make a run for it,
turn to page **90**.

To try to scare the jaguar away,
turn to page **91**.

You don't think moving Maria would be a good idea. Instead you'll try to help her here. First you dig through the supplies scattered throughout the wreckage. You find the cooler Maria kept filled with beverages and snacks. You open a bottle of water and bring it to Maria's lips.

She drinks only a little. She is moaning softly. Despite the intense heat, she's not sweating. That's a problem. Without sweat, her body has no way to cool itself. You pour some water on your T-shirt and dab her face with it, hoping that will help.

Turn the page.

As the day drags on, the cockpit gets hotter and hotter. The metal traps the heat. You realize you've made a mistake. You should have moved Maria out of here right away. Maybe there's still time.

Treatment of heatstroke if emergency medical care isn't immediately available

- Move the person to a shaded, cool area.

- Have the person lie down with his or her feet slightly elevated.

- Remove the person's clothing.

- Wrap the person in a wet cloth or apply wet cloths to the person's neck, armpits, and groin to help reduce his or her body temperature.

- Have the person drink water or another beverage slowly. Do not give him or her beverages that contain alcohol or caffeine.

Maria is unresponsive now. You have to drag her outside. You put her in a shaded spot and fan her with large leaves, hoping to bring down her body temperature. You go back inside to get more water. When you come back out, Maria isn't breathing anymore. You've lost her.

You shed a few tears, but you don't have much time for grieving. Staying alive has to be your only goal. You know a rescue effort must be out by now. If there are aircraft nearby, you have to get their attention.

To try to fix the plane's radio, turn to page 93.

To try building a signal fire, turn to page 96.

There's no way you're staying out here with a jaguar nearby. The cockpit is only about 20 feet away. If you get inside, you'll be safe.

"Come on," you whisper, helping Maria to her feet. She puts an arm around your shoulder so you can support her weight. You start to run.

You're almost to the plane when a huge weight crashes into you from behind. You hear Maria scream as you fall to the ground. You should have known better. Running is the last thing you want to do when a big cat is on the prowl.

Your last thought is of Maria. You hope she makes it out alive. You know you won't.

THE END

To follow another path, turn to page 11.
To read the conclusion, turn to page 101.

You can't outrun a jaguar. And you know that big cats can smell blood and have a natural instinct to chase anything that moves. Your best chance is to scare the jaguar away.

You stand and shout. You wave your arms and shake tree branches. Maria joins in, screaming weakly and beating a stick against the ground. Between the two of you, you make quite a racket.

The strategy works. You don't see or hear any sign of the jaguar again. It seems to have wandered away in search of quieter prey.

With sunset, the wreckage of the airplane has cooled off. It makes a perfect camp for the night. You sleep deeply, feeling safe for the first time since the crash.

Turn the page.

By morning Maria's condition has improved. She's not ready to do any physical work, but she says she can work on the radio while you search for food. When you return with an armful of inga fruits, you find her resting. She's already fixed the radio and called for help. "They'll be here within a few hours," she says, forcing a weak smile.

Your ordeal is almost over. Your quick thinking and courage have gotten you through three days in the jungle. You can hardly wait to tell your friends all about it.

THE END

To follow another path, turn to page 11.
To read the conclusion, turn to page 101.

The plane's radio is your best hope. If you can get it working, rescue teams should be able to find you easily. You head into the cockpit and get to work. You spend hours tinkering with the radio, connecting and reconnecting wires, fiddling with dials, and finally just banging on it. Nothing works. Maybe Maria could have fixed it, but it's beyond your skills. You sigh, realizing that you've wasted most of the day.

A plane's radio may still work, even after a crash.

Turn the page.

The sun is close to setting. You have to gather firewood quickly. As you hack through the heavy vegetation, you feel a sting on your leg. You look down and see a red welt starting to form. Something bit you! You hobble back to camp for a better look. The painful welt is getting bigger. Soon you start to lose feeling in your leg.

You don't know what bit you. It could have been a snake or a venomous bug. Or maybe it was a scorpion sting. Whatever it was, it had strong venom. With each moment you feel worse. Your body feels as if it's on fire. Finally you black out. Your last thought is that you survived the plane crash only to be killed by some tiny jungle creature.

THE END

To follow another path, turn to page 11.
To read the conclusion, turn to page 101.

The sting of some scorpions contains enough venom to kill a person.

The best way to attract attention is lots and lots of smoke. The sun is still fairly high in the sky, so this is a good time to build a signal fire. You choose a spot of cleared-out jungle along the path where the plane came down.

Starting your fire is easy. Maria had a lighter in the plane. You use it to burn the pages from a newspaper she had in her pack. From there, you get the wood burning. You add plenty of branches and small logs, getting a huge flame.

You dig around for damp wood and green plants. They are full of water, which means that they'll release lots of heavy smoke when they burn.

A smoky fire is easily spotted from the air.

You pile on damp wood and leaves. Huge plumes of smoke rise above the jungle canopy. In less than an hour you hear the sound you've been waiting for. It's the thump-thump-thump of spinning helicopter blades. Someone has spotted your signal fire!

Turn the page.

Rescue workers are trained to help in emergency situations.

The rescue helicopter finds an open space to touch down. You rush to meet it. You're filled with relief that you've survived your jungle ordeal.

At the same time, you feel terrible that you weren't able to save Maria. You know that your decision not to get her outside will haunt you for the rest of your life.

THE END

To follow another path, turn to page 11.
To read the conclusion, turn to page 101.

Danger lurks on land and in the water in the Amazon jungle.

CHAPTER 5

Surviving the Jungle

The jungle might seem like a great place for an adventure. But as you've read, it's full of danger. Big predators such as black caimans and jaguars are only the beginning. Insects, spiders, scorpions, snakes, and other crawling things can be even more dangerous. Even microscopic organisms living in jungle waters can be deadly.

Survival in high-stress situations starts in your mind. The most important thing is keeping the will to live. You need to stay calm. Panic leads to bad decisions. When your life is on the line with every choice you make, you need to have a cool, clear thought process. And you must always remain positive. Stay focused on the goals of staying alive and finding help. You can never give up, no matter how grim the situation gets.

Next you have to assess your situation. Are you hurt? Are you in any immediate danger? Are rescuers going to be looking for you? Will they know where to look? These questions will help decide your survival strategy. Do you need to stay put or search for help? Where can you find food, water, and shelter?

The jungle can be a scary place. Staying calm and using common sense are your best bets for survival.

Finding the right answers to these questions can be the difference between life and death. People often have to do difficult things in order to stay alive. Could you eat bugs if you had to? Would you have the courage to climb aboard a log raft on a river filled with dangerous predators? Could you keep going, even when it felt as if there was no hope of rescue?

Many hidden dangers lurk in the water. Building a raft can help keep you safe.

If you can answer "yes" to all of these questions, you might have what it takes to survive a situation like the one in this book. Of course no one would choose to be alone in the jungle fighting for survival. But it's nice to know that if it ever happened to you, you'd know what to do to give yourself the best possible chance of getting out alive.

REAL SURVIVORS

1944–1972—Nine Japanese soldiers, including Shoichi Yokoi, fled into the jungles of Guam after the Japanese lost a World War II battle to the United States. Yokoi alone survived the final eight years. Yokoi hunted, fished, and gathered fruit. He lived in a cave. He boiled all of his water before drinking it. Yokoi was found in 1972, but even then he resisted being brought back to civilization. He believed that it was dishonorable for a Japanese soldier to be captured, even long after the war ended.

December 1971—Juliane Köpcke, a 17-year-old student, was the only survivor of an airplane crash over the jungle of Peru. Despite falling more than two miles, Köpcke somehow survived with only a broken collarbone, a concussion, and cuts and bruises. But her cuts quickly become infested with maggots and other parasites. She discovered a stream and followed it downstream, remembering the advice her father had once given her. After 10 days, she finally came across a small boat and a hut. She stayed there until lumberjacks found her the next day and were able to get her to safety.

December 1981—A young backpacker named Yossi Ghinsberg was separated from his group in the jungle of Bolivia. Riding a crude log raft down a river, he survived a plummet over a waterfall. For the next three weeks, Ghinsberg struggled to survive and find rescue. He was attacked by termites, survived an encounter with a jaguar, and freed himself from chest-deep quicksand before finally being rescued.

November 2007—Hikers Guilhem Nayral and Loïc Pillois became lost on a hike in the Amazon. They chose to wait for rescue and built a makeshift camp. Their main sources of food during the ordeal included beetles and tarantula spiders. They heard helicopters overhead, but no rescue came. The men stayed there for almost seven weeks before deciding to head out again in search of civilization. On the journey, a venomous spider bit Nayral. He stayed behind to tend to his wound. Pillois went on ahead, found rescue, and came back for Nayral.

August 2008—Hiker Hayden Adcock survived 11 days alone in the jungle of Laos. Adcock was in bad condition when rescuers reached him by helicopter. He had serious infections from drinking impure water. His skin was covered with wounds from flesh-eating lizards. Maggots had burrowed into many of the wounds. Adcock suffered multiple organ failures and was perhaps just hours away from death. With medical care, though, he recovered.

SURVIVAL QUIZ

1. If you run into a jaguar or other big cat, what's the best thing to do?

A. Throw things at it.

B. Stand your ground, wave your arms, and shout.

C. Turn your back, and run as fast as you can.

2. What is the best kind of wood to use for a signal fire?

A. Use only dry wood, which burns quickly.

B. Use a combination of dry wood to burn and wet wood to create smoke.

C. It doesn't matter what kind of wood you use.

3. What is the best way to purify river or stream water for drinking?

A. Use a fire to heat the water.

B. Use a cloth as a filter to remove any parasites.

C. Let it set in a container for several hours until the parasites settle to the bottom.

Answers: B, B, A

READ MORE

Campbell, Guy. *The Boys' Book of Survival: How to Survive Anything, Anywhere.* New York: Scholastic, 2009.

Long, Denise. *Survivor Kid: A Practical Guide to Wilderness Survival.* Chicago: Chicago Review Press, 2011.

O'Shei, Tim. *How to Survive in the Wilderness.* Mankato, Minn.: Capstone Press, 2009.

INTERNET SITES

Use FactHound to find Internet sites related to this book. All of the sites on FactHound have been researched by our staff.

Here's all you do:
Visit *www.facthound.com*
Type in this code: 9781429665889

GLOSSARY

caiman (KAY-muhn)—a Central and South American reptile closely related to alligators

canopy (KAN-uh-pee)—the top level of vegetation in a forest

concussion (kuhn-KUSH-uhn)—an injury to the brain caused by a blow to the head

dehydration (dee-hye-DRAY-shuhn)—a life-threatening medical condition caused by a lack of water

flash flood (FLASH FLUHD)—a sudden flood that comes with little warning, usually as the result of heavy rainfall

heatstroke (HEETSTROHK)—a life-threatening medical condition caused by prolonged heat exposure

inga (ing-UH)—a tropical fruit that tastes like vanilla ice cream and grows in long pods

parasite (PA-ruh-site)—an organism that lives on or inside a person or animal

peccary (PEH-kuh-ree)—a type of wild pig

rain forest (RAYN FOR-ist)—a forest that gets a great deal of annual rainfall

tropical (TROP-uh-kuhl)—existing in the area of Earth near the equator

venom (VEN-uhm)—a poison transmitted by the bite or sting of an animal

BIBLIOGRAPHY

Fears, J. Wayne. *The Complete Book of Outdoor Survival.* Iola, Wis.: Krause Publications, 1999.

Grylls, Bear. *Man Vs. Wild: Survival Techniques from the Most Dangerous Places on Earth.* New York: Hyperion Books, 2008.

McNab, Chris. *Special Forces Survival Guide: Wilderness Survival Skills from the World's Most Elite Military Units.* New York: MJF Books, 2011.

Oldfield, Sara. *Rainforest.* Cambridge, Mass.: MIT Press, 2003.

Stroud, Les. *Survive!: Essential Skills and Tactics to Get You Out of Anywhere—Alive.* New York: Collins, 2008.

Towell, Colin. *The Survival Handbook: Essential Skills for Outdoor Adventure.* New York: DK Publishing, 2009.

INDEX